Child Soldiers

Linda Barghoorn

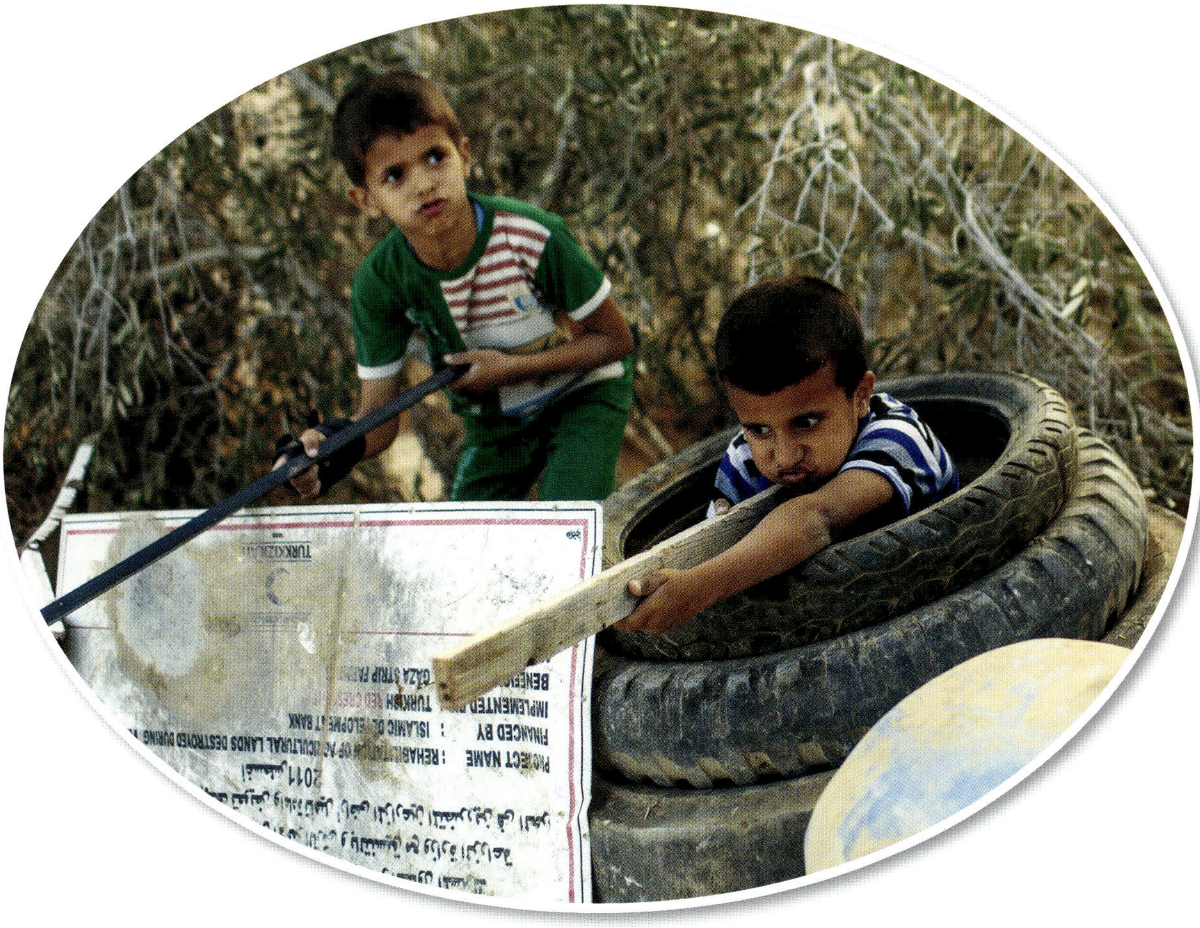

A Crabtree Forest Book

Crabtree Publishing
crabtreebooks.com

Author: Linda Barghoorn

Series research and development:
Ellen Rodger and Janine Deschenes

Editorial director: Kathy Middleton

Editor: Ellen Rodger

Proofreader: Melissa Boyce

Design: Samara Parent

IMAGE CREDITS

Shutterstock:
Adriana Mahdalova: p 39; akramalrasny: pp 12-13, p 36; Alucardion: p 19; anasalhajj: front cover, p 31, 37 (bottom); cemT: p 26 (top), 32 (bottom); Dereje: p 33 (bottom); Drop of Light: p 27 (bottom); ehasdemir: p 43; Everett Collection: p 6, 15 (left); Friemann: p 29 (bottom); gary yim: p 18 (bottom); Jayakri: p 10 (bottom); kafeinkolik: p 32 (top); lev radin: p 37 (top); mehmet ali poyraz: title page, p 38 (bottom); Mostofa Mohiuddin: p 40; oliverdelahaye: p 27 (top), 29 (top); Orlok: p 44 (bottom); paintings: p 41 (top); Phil Pasquini: p 45 (bottom); PradeepGaurs: p 24; Pres Panayotov: p 41 (bottom); punghi: p 4; quetions123: p 25; R. Bociaga: p 18 (middle); Richard Juilliart: p 11, 14, 18 (top); robertonencini: p 17 (bottom); Trent Inness: p 26 (bottom), 35; Vladimir Melnik: p 5 (top); Wandering views: p 44 (top)

Wikimedia Commons:
Bundesarchiv, Bild 183-G0627-500-001 / CC-BY-SA 3.0: p 20 (top); Charles W. Alexander: p22; Iran-Iraq war-gallery: p 21 (middle); L. Rose: p 20 (bottom); Michelle Campbell, CEO, St Joseph's Health Care Foundation, London Ontario: p 33 (top); Public Domain: p 15 (right); Udoweier: p 17 (top)

Crabtree Publishing

crabtreebooks.com   800-387-7650
Copyright © 2024 Crabtree Publishing

All rights reserved. No part of this publication may be reproduced, stored in a retrieval system or be transmitted in any form or by any means, electronic, mechanical, photocopying, recording, or otherwise, without the prior written permission of Crabtree Publishing Company.
In Canada: We acknowledge the financial support of the Government of Canada through the Canada Book Fund for our publishing activities.

Hardcover	978-1-0398-1527-8
Paperback	978-1-0398-1553-7
Ebook (pdf)	978-1-0398-1605-3
Epub	978-1-0398-1579-7

Published in Canada
Crabtree Publishing
616 Welland Avenue
St. Catharines, Ontario
L2M 5V6

Published in the United States
Crabtree Publishing
347 Fifth Avenue
Suite 1402-145
New York, New York, 10016

Library and Archives Canada Cataloguing in Publication
Available at Library and Archives Canada

Library of Congress Cataloging-in-Publication Data
Available at the Library of Congress

Printed in the U.S.A./072023/CG20230214

CONTENTS

Introduction 4

Chapter One
Children as Soldiers 6

Chapter Two
Recruitment of Children 14

Chapter Three
Protecting the Rights of Children 22

Chapter Four
Lives Forever Changed 30

Chapter Five
Rehabilitation and Reintegration 36

Wrap-Up
Looking to the Future 42

Glossary 46

Stay Informed 47

Index 48

Introduction

Ibrahim was just 14 when he and four of his friends were captured from their village by armed rebel soldiers in South Sudan. The rebels killed Ibrahim's mother as she tried to stop them. The boys were forced to march for days through the bush with only a few hours of sleep each night and almost nothing to eat or drink. Finally, they arrived at the rebel camp and were brought before the rebel leader. He warned them not to try to escape. "Forget your families," he told them. "You are soldiers now."

Thousands of children are forced into conflicts each year. Around 250,000 child soldiers—some as young as eight or nine years of age—are participating in conflicts around the world today. Some have been forced to serve in their country's military. Others join rebel groups, **militias**, or gangs to fight against their country's leaders and the social and **political systems** they represent.

A child in Sanaa, Yemen, plays with a toy gun. Civil war broke out in the Arabian Peninsula country in 2014. The United Nations (UN) estimates that roughly 3,500 children in Yemen have been **recruited** into rebel militias.

CURRENT WORLD CONFLICTS

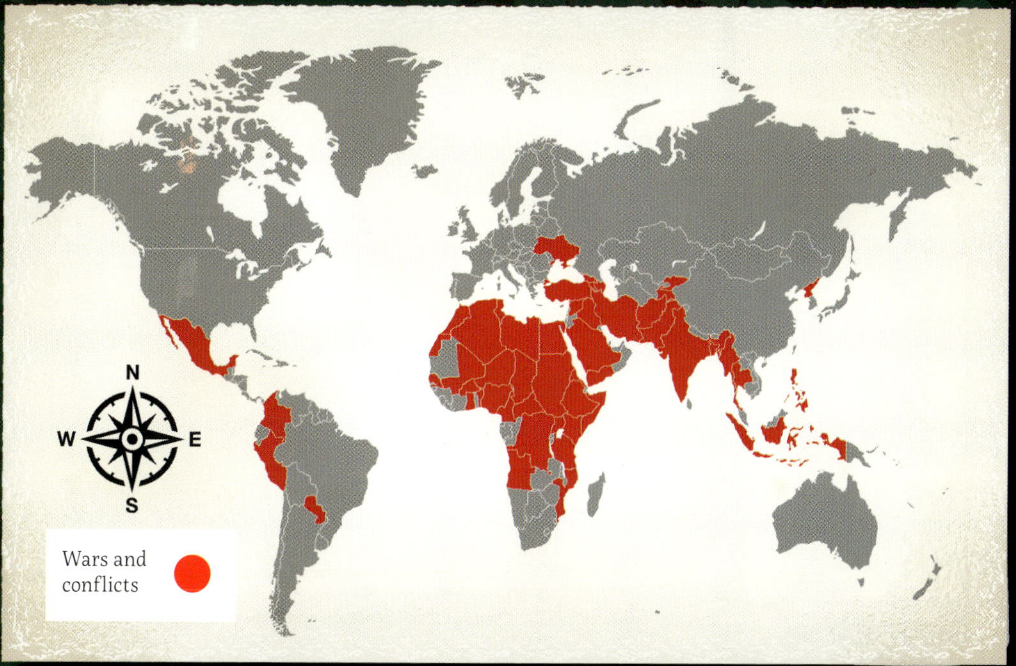

Wars and conflicts

Children as Soldiers

For much of human history, conflicts have been fought by soldiers who voluntarily joined armies to fight their enemies. Regular citizens—the elderly, disabled, women, and children—were generally not expected to officially take part. But they did.

Children have been used in conflicts since the days of the ancient Roman army. During the American Civil War (1861–1865), a number of teenagers were granted medals for their roles in assisting in the military. In **World War II** (1939–1945), thousands of German boys were **indoctrinated**, or taught to accept and follow **Nazi beliefs**. Near the end of the war, many older boys were also conscripted, or selected and required by their country to fight on the European battlefields alongside adult men.

Hitler Youth was the Nazi Party's youth organization. From 1936 to 1945, it was the only official youth organization for boys in Germany and German territories. It taught and promoted Nazi beliefs and prepared children to be soldiers.

More Violent over Time

The use of child soldiers is not new, but the practice of using children in conflicts has become more **deliberate** and violent. Children have become a common weapon of war in many conflict zones around the world. Child soldiers are encouraged to be cruel to others and are often beaten by the adults who train them.

Children have been fighters in conflicts all over the world. Some of those conflicts are wars between countries, while others are civil wars, or wars between opposing groups in the same country. Children are also used as **enforcers** and soldiers for gangs and **cartels** fighting to control the drug trade throughout North, Central, and South America, Europe, and Asia.

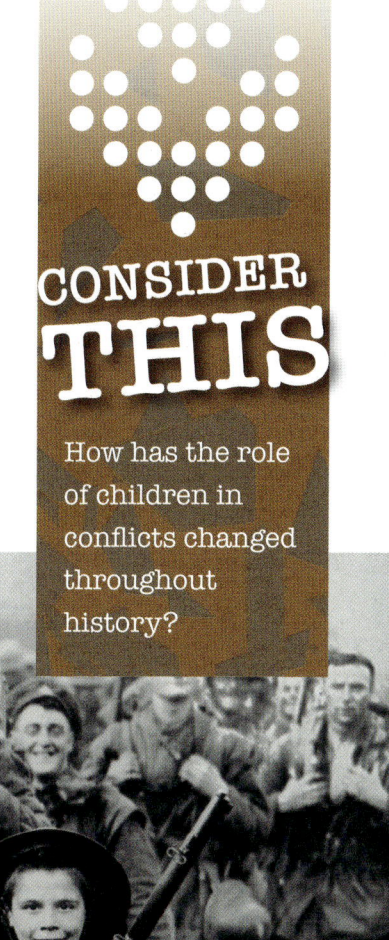

CONSIDER THIS

How has the role of children in conflicts changed throughout history?

A young boy carries a British soldier's rifle as troops liberate, or free, a city in France from German control during **World War I** (1914–1918). Many teenage boys filled the ranks of the British Army during that war. Even today, the armed forces of the United Kingdom recruits minors, or people under the age of 18.

What Is a Child Soldier?

A child soldier is a child below the age of 18, who plays any kind of role as a member of an armed force or armed group. Many child soldiers are forced to take part in actual fighting. Others are used as scouts to prepare the way for ambush attacks or as local messengers. They may work as guards, porters, or bodyguards for senior **commanders**. Or they may be trained to care for weapons, make bombs, or sweep for land mines. About four in 10 child soldiers are girls, who are often enslaved or forced to become the wives of male soldiers.

Soldiers in major conflicts such as World War I were often very young. Many armies accepted recruits as young as 16, but it was not unusual for a boy of 12 or 14 to tell recruiting officers that he was older.

Chapter One: Children as Soldiers

PERSPECTIVES

Cyril Jose, World War I Child Soldier

Cyril was just 15 when he joined the British Army during World War I. He was a tin-miner's son from Cornwall—a poor rural area in southern England. The war in Europe seemed a world and an adventure away. Cyril enlisted, even though he was legally too young. But if you were healthy and physically fit you were often accepted. When he received his army rifle, he wrote an excited letter to his sister. But by the end of the war, having witnessed incredible suffering on the French battlefields, Cyril became a strong opponent of war.

World War I was known for its brutal trench warfare, which involved ditches dug as protective cover on the battlefields. Soldiers lived, slept, and ate in the cold and uncomfortable trenches.

Why Are Children Targeted?

Children are targeted for recruitment as soldiers for a number of reasons. They have not fully developed a clear sense of right and wrong, which makes it easier to **manipulate** and control them than adults. Because they do not have a well-developed sense of danger, it is easier to convince them to perform dangerous roles as fighters, suicide bombers, and mine sweepers.

Children are less expensive to feed and shelter than adults. And for many dishonest leaders in conflicts, children are expendable—they can simply be replaced if they are injured or killed. Modern weapons have become cheaper and easier to carry than the cannons and arms of the past. So, children can be easily trained to use and carry them.

Sometimes children are trained early to protect their families during conflict. They may learn how to use weapons. Some must look after siblings or find food.

A Russian teenager assembles an automatic weapon during a military sports competition for youth.

Chapter One: Children as Soldiers

About one in six children—more than 350 million—currently live in a conflict zone. Often these are in poor countries, where children are especially vulnerable to recruitment and **radicalization** by corrupt armed forces, rebel groups, or other armed groups.

A young boy in Juba, South Sudan, gives a military salute while holding a toy gun.

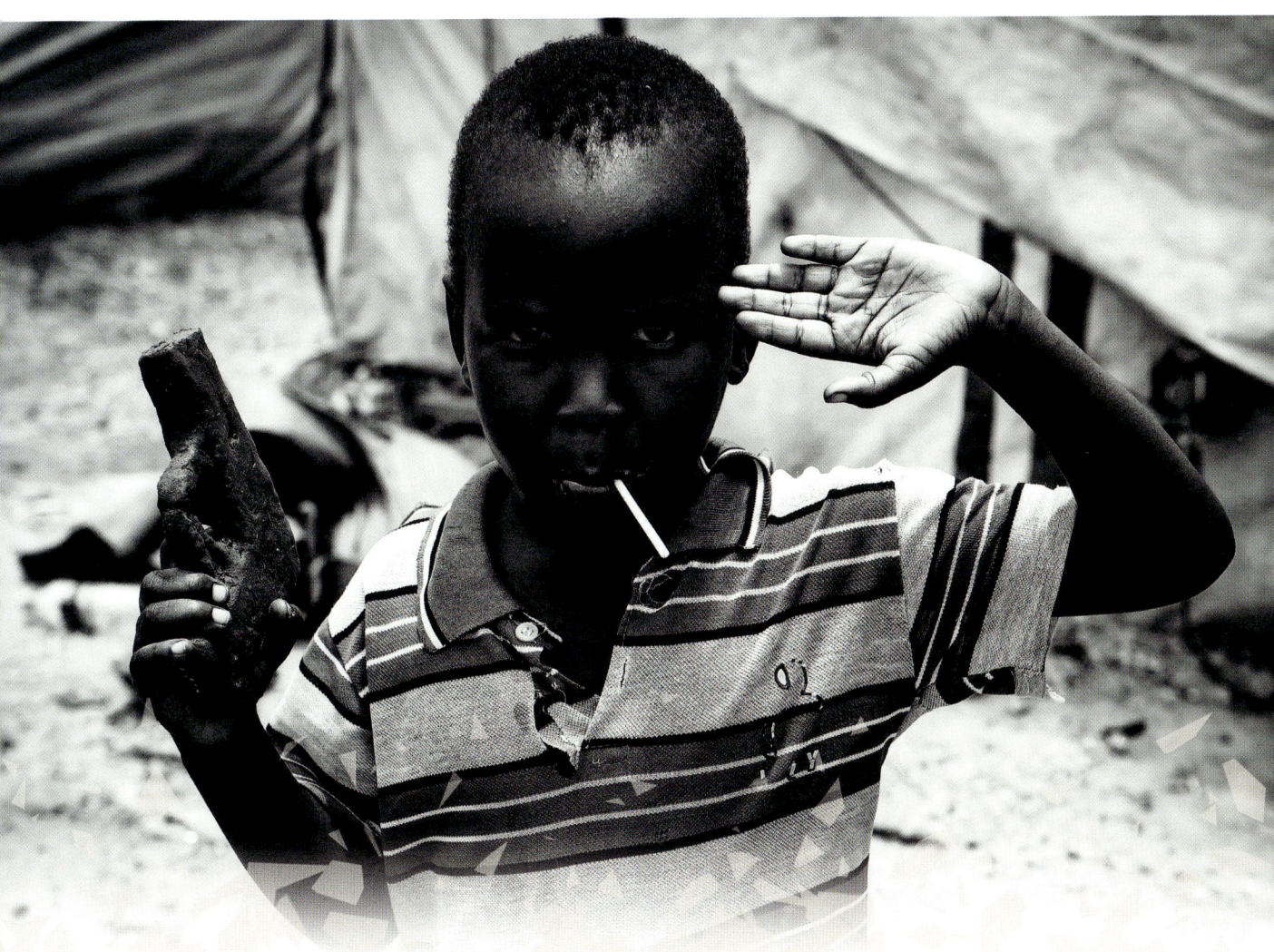

> *Man has created the ultimate cheap, expendable, yet sophisticated weapon, at the expense of humanity's own future: its children...*
>
> GENERAL ROMÉO DALLAIRE,
> "PLIGHT OF THE CHILD SOLDIER," WORLD VISION,
> OCTOBER 2020

PERSPECTIVES

Ricky Richard Anywar, Child Soldier to Humanitarian

Ricky Richard Anywar was 14 when he was forced to watch as his family was killed by soldiers in the Lord's Resistance Army (LRA), a **militant** group fighting the Ugandan government. For the next two years, he was forced to fight as an LRA soldier and regularly witnessed torture and killing. Finally, he escaped when he was 16. Later, he founded Friends of Orphans, an organization that provides former child soldiers with therapy and education to help them **reintegrate** into their community. Ricky received the World of Children Humanitarian Award for his work.

> *I saw torture, rape, killing, abductions...and all before I was 17.*
>
> RICKY RICHARD ANYWAR,
> 2008 WORLD OF CHILDREN HUMANITARIAN AWARD

Chapter One: Children as Soldiers

Life of Danger

Life as a child soldier is full of danger. Often children are deprived of food and healthy living conditions in order to manipulate them into obeying orders from their commanders. Some are given drugs or alcohol to dull the fear or pain, often leading to lifelong addiction. Others become so **desensitized** to violence and abuse that it is extremely difficult to return to a normal life in their community—even if they can escape soldiering. Many are injured, disabled, sexually assaulted, or killed. Girls, in particular, are at constant risk of gender-based violence (GBV). GBV is physical and/or sexual abuse.

Children and youths living in conflict areas are easy prey for groups that want to use them as child soldiers. Sometimes they are scooped up and forced into fighting. Others may be enticed into joining armed groups because their homes are destroyed or their families have been killed and they have few options for survival.

Chapter Two

Recruitment of Children

Trapped in conflict regions, children become participants in armed conflict for a number of reasons. Some are recruited by force—physically abducted, or stolen, or threatened into joining by armed groups or forces. Others "choose" to take part.

For children joining a conflict, "choice" is often not freely made and not fully understood. Most children have no real understanding of what they will be expected to take part in. Many children are forced by extreme poverty or insecurity into becoming child soldiers in order to survive.

Sometimes children are given up by their families in exchange for protection from local armed groups. Some join the conflict to take revenge for a family member who has been killed. For others, belonging to a group, even an abusive and dangerous one, brings a sense of belonging that they may not have had in their own community.

The promise of food and security is a powerful weapon used by armed leaders when recruiting children.

Socialized for Conflict

In all cultures, children and youths are socialized, or trained to behave or participate in society in a certain way. In World War I, the British Army recruited 250,000 boys under the age of 18. Some joined to be patriotic. Others were shamed into joining. The general feeling was that everyone had to do their part for victory. This influenced many boys into joining their country's armed forces.

(below) Patriotism, or a strong love and support of a person's country, is powerful during wartime. It can motivate and urge youths and children to prove their loyalty.

(above) At 12 years old, Sidney Lewis was the youngest British soldier in WWI. He enlisted without his parents' knowledge and fought in several major battles before his mother demanded he be released.

CONSIDER THIS

How are children manipulated into taking part in conflicts? Do you think they understand what they are being asked to do? Why or why not?

Children into Soldiers

Transforming a child into an efficient soldier can be done in many ways, beyond appealing to pride or patriotism. Child soldiers who are abducted or indoctrinated may be coerced, or persuaded through threats. This includes being deprived of food, shelter, or security. They may be given drugs or alcohol to desensitize them to the violent acts they are ordered to commit.

Abuse is an important strategy in creating a human who becomes numb to the violence they are forced to perform. As a child becomes dependent on the group for their survival, they are less likely to try to escape.

Fear and threats are used to condition child soldiers, or make them behave in a certain way. Their commanders want them to be totally obedient so that they will obey orders and not question their authority.

Chapter Two: Recruitment of Children

PERSPECTIVES

Ishmael Beah now lives in the United States and is a well-known human rights activist.

Ishmael Beah, Author

In 1991, a brutal civil war in Sierra Leone, in western Africa, changed Ishmael Beah's life. His parents were killed when armed rebels invaded their village. Ishmael fled, but within months he was forced to become a child soldier for the government army when he was 13. His commanders got him addicted to drugs and brainwashed him into committing incredible acts of violence, which he can never forget. It took him three years to escape and several more to **rehabilitate**. As an adult, he has written a book about his experiences, and two fiction novels.

Child soldiers don't get the chance to develop and play like other children. They are also deprived of formal schooling.

 *My squad was my family, my gun was my provider and protector, and my rule was to kill or be killed.*

Ishmael Beah,
A Long Way Gone: Memoirs of a Boy Soldier

Who Recruits Children?

International law forbids the use of children under the age of 18 as soldiers in any armed conflict. Many countries have signed a treaty that upholds this agreement. But the practice of recruiting and training children as soldiers, by both armed forces and armed groups, has continued.

Armed forces—the military forces of a country—are governed by these international laws, which are designed to hold them accountable, or responsible, for any violations. But when wars escalate, it can be tempting for governments and military leaders to put aside their commitments to international law to win a conflict. They may employ more desperate warfare tactics, including the use of children as soldiers.

In the conflict between armed rebel forces and the government military in Colombia, children were often used as guards for the government military. They were called "little bells." Rebel groups, on the other hand, nicknamed them "little bees" because they could quickly "sting" their enemies during attacks.

A soldier in the armed forces of South Sudan lights a candle to celebrate independence from Sudan. Both sides recruited child soldiers in conflicts, including two civil wars.

The armed forces of the Southeast Asian country of Myanmar has an enlistment age of 18. However, army officials have been known to recruit boys under age 18.

Chapter Two: Recruitment of Children

Armed groups—often militants or rebels—are separate from the armed forces of a country. They represent the majority of groups responsible for recruiting child soldiers. Because they often operate outside of legal boundaries, they are much harder to hold responsible for their actions.

Boko Haram is a terrorist organization that operates mostly in northeastern Nigeria and other Central and West African countries. It carries out massacres, bombings, and kidnappings of children. In 2014, 276 schoolgirls were kidnapped from the town of Chibok and enslaved. Their families pressured the government to get them back.

 **CONSIDER THIS** What is the difference between an armed force and an armed group? What kind of laws regulate, or control, their behavior?

Warlords and Other Leaders

Leaders of both governments of countries and rebel armed groups have been responsible for recruiting children into conflicts. Often they do so to serve their own personal ambitions. Holding them responsible has proven difficult, despite the international laws and criminal courts that are designed to do so.

Before World War II, Germany's Nazi government created a youth league—the Hitler Youth—named for their leader Adolf Hitler. These children were indoctrinated with Nazi beliefs. During the war, thousands were conscripted into the military. Those who refused to serve would not be allowed to attend secondary school.

Sixteen-year-old Hitler Youth Willi Hübner receives the Iron Cross during WWII. This was one way in which Adolf Hitler tried to inspire Germany's children to become war heroes.

Former child soldiers from the Democratic Republic of the Congo (DRC). They were known as *kadogos*, or "little ones," when they were forced to join militias and armies.

Chapter Two: Recruitment of Children

Saddam Hussein, Iraq's leader from 1979 to 2003, enlisted boys between 10 and 15 years old into *Ashbal Saddam*—or Saddam's Lion Cubs. This was a group that trained youths to be fighters. Many Cubs went on to fight in the military as teens and adults. Iraq was known to have several youth soldier units. Some fought in the Iran-Iraq War (1980–1988). During that war, Iranian boys 12 and up were recruited into the *Basij*. This was a volunteer **paramilitary** force that fought along with adult men in the army.

A child soldier of the Iran-Iraq War. Iranian children were also sent to clear minefields during the war. Some wore symbolic keys around their necks to guarantee their entrance to heaven should they be killed. Iran's leader claimed their sacrifices were a necessary part of the war.

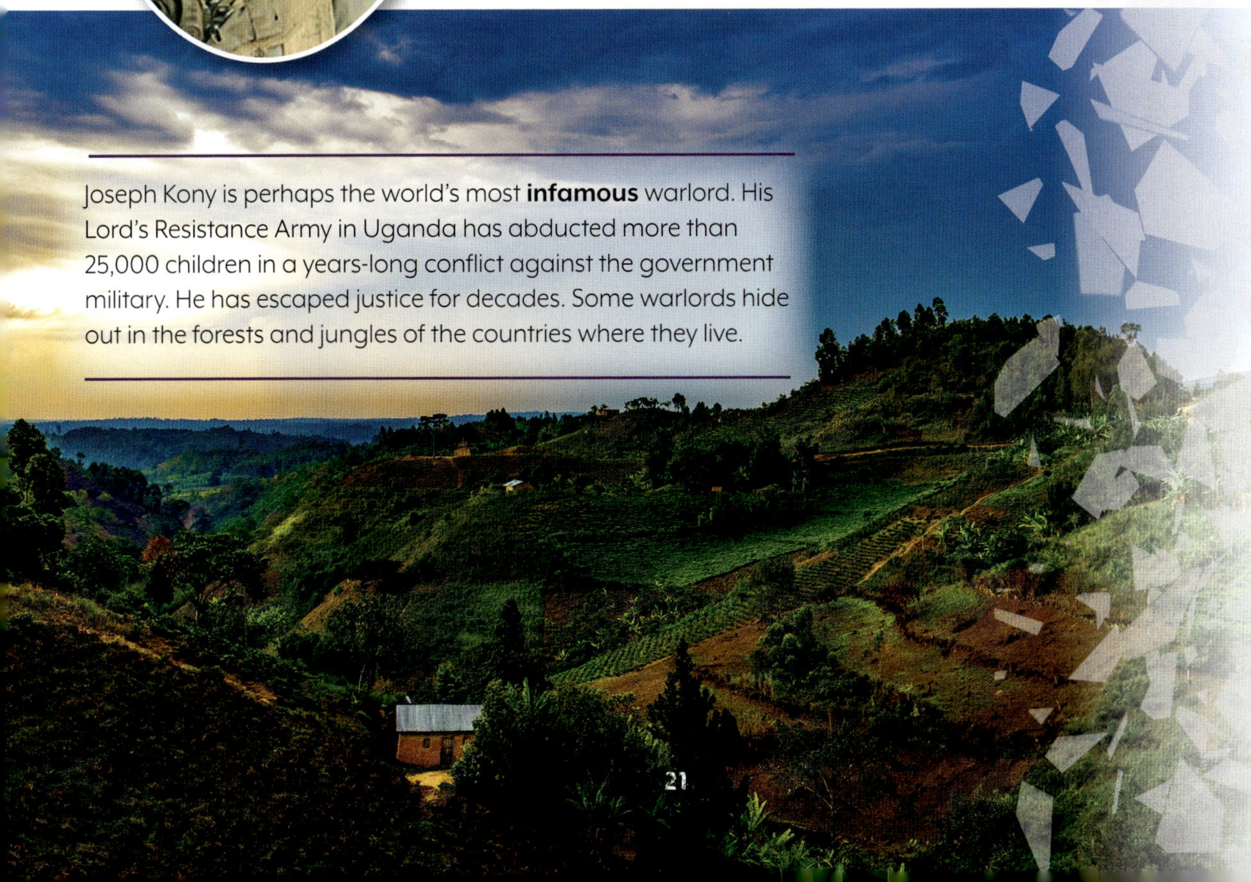

Joseph Kony is perhaps the world's most **infamous** warlord. His Lord's Resistance Army in Uganda has abducted more than 25,000 children in a years-long conflict against the government military. He has escaped justice for decades. Some warlords hide out in the forests and jungles of the countries where they live.

Chapter Three

Protecting the Rights of Children

Children are especially vulnerable during times of conflict. A number of international laws and conventions have been created to provide protection to children in conflict zones.

After the enormous casualties of World War II, there was a strong desire to find ways to help reduce the suffering of people during conflicts. International humanitarian law is a set of laws created to protect people in conflict regions and regulate the behavior of governments and leaders in conflicts. It was created as a result of the 1949 Geneva Conventions. This is a series of treaties that outline wartime principles for the treatment of civilians, soldiers, and prisoners of war.

Evidence from the Nuremberg trials held after World War II. These criminal trials were the first to hold individual people responsible for war crimes and crimes against humanity. They helped establish international criminal law.

The Geneva Conventions prohibit the recruitment and use of children under the age of 18 in any kind of conflict. They work to ensure that children's needs for food, medical assistance, and shelter in conflict zones are provided for. Children separated from their families during conflicts must be protected until they can be returned to their families.

CONSIDER THIS

Why was international humanitarian law created and why is it so important?

Two women walk through the rubble that was their home in England after a World War II bombing raid.

Rights for Children

Probably the most important set of rules ever created to protect children was the United Nations Convention on the Rights of the Child (UNCRC). It was adopted in 1989. It is the most widely ratified, or agreed-upon, treaty in history. A total of 194 countries adopted the convention as law.

There are 54 convention articles, or rules, listed to help protect children. Article 38 dictates that governments are responsible for protecting children from violence and recruitment into conflicts. Article 39 says that children have the right to get help if they have been hurt or affected by war so they can recover their health and dignity. Each UN member state is responsible for ensuring that these articles are upheld.

Afghan children outside the United Nations High Commissioner for Refugees office in New Delhi, India. They are protesting conflict and rights violations in their country and asking for the right to **refugee** status.

Chapter Three: Protecting the Rights of Children

Eleven years after the UNCRC was adopted, the UN Security Council added an additional **Protocol** to the convention. It banned the recruitment and use of children under the age of 18 in armed conflict. Despite the creation of these international laws, eliminating the recruitment of child soldiers has proved difficult.

Generations of children, like this Palestinian child, live in refugee camps throughout the world because of armed conflict. Their lack of security and the violence that surrounds them makes them more vulnerable to recruitment into armed groups.

> *Throughout the world hundreds of thousands of children go to sleep each night, not with their favorite teddybear or doll beside them, but with a gun.*
>
> Joint statement by Margot Wallström, Minister for Foreign Affairs of Sweden, and Leila Zerrougui, Special Representative of the Secretary-General for Children and Armed Conflict, "Ending the Use of Child Soldiers," February 12, 2017

25

Young boys play in a Turkish refugee camp.

Enforcing the Laws

The United Nations has continued to urge countries to support the protection of children during conflicts. In 2014, it supported the #ChildrenNotSoldiers campaign, designed to increase international support to end the recruitment of child soldiers. The #ACTtoProtect campaign was launched in 2019 to promote awareness about how children are impacted by war.

The International Committee of the Red Cross (ICRC) is the caretaker of international humanitarian law. The ICRC is responsible for providing humanitarian protection and assistance to victims of armed conflict. It also promotes international law and encourages countries to uphold their treaty obligations.

An Afghan child in a refugee camp. Nobody wants to live in a refugee camp, but many families go there seeking safety from conflict.

Chapter Three: Protecting the Rights of Children

The International Criminal Court (ICC) complements the work of UN member states' national courts. It is intended as the "court of last resort." This means it can only investigate and prosecute individuals accused of war crimes when national courts are unwilling to do so. The ICC has tried to bring individuals charged with recruiting child soldiers and committing war crimes against children to justice. The process can be long and difficult.

Inside the International Criminal Court in The Hague, Netherlands.

Workers uncover and identify bodies in a mass grave in Bucha, Ukraine, during Russia's invasion of that country in 2022. Forensic experts must carefully record and preserve evidence of war crimes. Often, trials are not held until many years later.

Seeking Justice

International courts and laws are only effective if countries and groups agree to be bound by their rules. The ICC has limited powers to arrest armed groups who recruit children as soldiers. In countries where conflict is ongoing, it can be difficult even to find and arrest an individual charged with recruiting children. Some UN member countries have refused to uphold rulings by the ICC because they feel the court is biased against them.

Armed rebel groups often have little respect for international law. They rarely respond to sanctions or charges against them. They are not motivated to release child soldiers because doing so only exposes them to the risk of arrest and punishment.

Children are always among the civilian victims of war. An average of 25 children are killed or injured in conflicts every day. The Save the Children charity says 93,236 children were hurt or killed from 2010 to 2019.

 What institutions are responsible for upholding international humanitarian law and bringing criminals to justice? What are some of the challenges they face?

Chapter Three: Protecting the Rights of Children

PERSPECTIVES

Fatou Bensouda is a lawyer from the West African country of Gambia.

Fatou Bensouda, War Crimes Prosecutor

Fatou Bensouda served as a prosecutor with the ICC from 2012 to 2021. She was the first woman and first African to serve in this role. During her term she directed 14 investigations of criminals accused of war crimes, including people accused of recruiting child soldiers. She said she was committed to giving a voice to voiceless victims. In 2021, she and her office were nominated for the Nobel Peace Prize for their work.

Since the ICC was created in 2002, only five people have been convicted of war crimes. Some, like Jean-Pierre Bemba Gombo, have had their convictions reversed. Others have never been brought to justice.

Chapter Four

Lives Forever Changed

In their role as soldiers, children are exposed to extreme forms of violence. They may be forced to witness violent acts or to participate in them. They often become victims of violence at the hands of their commanders.

Many child soldiers are forced to take part in violent training exercises or initiation ceremonies. These are designed to numb the child to the brutality they will experience as a soldier and to break the child's emotional ties with their family and community.

The emotional scars that result make it very difficult for a child soldier to live a normal life when they gain freedom.

30

This kind of trauma will have long-term effects on the child's physical and emotional health. Most will suffer from some form of post-traumatic stress disorder, or PTSD, which is a mental health condition triggered by a frightening event. It may cause flashbacks, nightmares, the inability to sleep, anger, depression, and anxiety.

Even if they "volunteer" to fight to defend their family or country, children and youths cannot know the future trauma they will suffer from their experiences. Some won't know that their later methods of coping, including using drugs or alcohol, are actually trauma responses.

Youths in Yemen patrol their neighborhoods and cities during that country's civil war.

> *Our innocence had been replaced by fear and we had become monsters. There was nothing we could do about it.*
>
> Ishmael Beah,
> *A Long Way Gone: Memoirs of a Boy Soldier*

Long-Term Consequences

The consequences of trauma on a child can last a lifetime. The violent loss of childhood and its innocence can leave emotional scars that, if not treated, can limit a child's ability to lead a healthy, happy, productive life as an adult. Some former child soldiers are abandoned by their families because of the violence they have committed.

Child soldiers must be fully rehabilitated and brought back into communities. Otherwise, they are more likely to rejoin an armed group. Rejoining means they repeat the cycle of violence and mistrust.

Sometimes child soldiers cannot return to their former homes. Home may not exist anymore. Their families may be displaced or in refugee camps. Or their families may be afraid of them.

Chapter Four: Lives Forever Changed

PERSPECTIVES

Roméo Dallaire suffers from PTSD from his mission in Rwanda. He is passionate about preventing and ending the use of child soldiers and has written a book on the subject.

Roméo Dallaire, Child Soldier Advocate

Retired Lieutenant-General Roméo Dallaire is the founder of the Dallaire Institute for Children, Peace, and Security. It was created to end the recruitment and use of children in conflicts. Previously he had a distinguished military career and led the UN peacekeeping mission in Rwanda during the 1994 Rwandan genocide. That was his first encounter with child soldiers and it shocked him. In 2002, Roméo Dallaire received Canada's World Peace Award for his work with children in conflicts.

The flame of remembrance marked the 20th anniversary of the Rwandan Genocide in 2014. The genocide was a period of mass killing by ethnic Hutu militias against the Tutsi **minority**. More than 600,000 people were killed in just over 100 days.

Rebuilding Lives

Recruiting children to participate in armed conflict is illegal. Most experts believe that children who are accused of crimes during conflicts should be considered victims, not criminals. Rather than charging children with a crime, efforts should focus on bringing the adult who recruited them to justice.

Arresting and charging child soldiers with war crimes will not help rebuild a country torn apart by war. Instead it is likely to further isolate child soldiers and their families. It creates **stigmas** that can limit a country's ability to rebuild and recover.

Chapter Four: Lives Forever Changed

Child Terrorists?

Children who have been recruited into armed groups that have been designated as terrorist groups are increasingly being arrested and charged as criminals and terrorists themselves. If children are to be put on trial for their actions, then laws must be adapted to help support former child soldiers. Any sentencing should be done with the goal of helping these children heal and reenter into society, rather than punishing them.

More than 1,000 children were detained for suspected links with the ISIS terrorist group by the government of Iraq in 2018.

CONSIDER THIS

Do you believe children should be punished for their actions as child soldiers? Why or why not?

> *Prosecutions should focus on the recruiters, not the children. What the children need is help rebuilding their lives.*
>
> Jo Becker,
> "Some Child Soldiers Get Rehabilitation, Others Get Prison,"
> Human Rights Watch, March 2019

35

Chapter Five

Rehabilitation and Reintegration

In countries that have been devastated by years of violent conflict, the needs of children must be considered above everything in order to build a strong, functioning society.

While the emotional trauma suffered by former child soldiers can seem overwhelming, most can recover with the proper care. Consistency and a commitment to long-term care are critical. Too often, a country recovering from conflict cannot help its children. Conflict may have isolated it, or left its people unable to operate without outside aid or help.

Yemeni children fill containers with safe water to bring back home. Bombs have destroyed buildings and services. Located in the Arabian Peninsula, Yemen has been suffering since civil war broke out in 2014.

PERSPECTIVES

Emmanuel Jal, Artist and Actor

Emmanuel Jal is a former child soldier from South Sudan. He has survived enormous trauma to become a successful recording artist and ambassador for peace and education. He has written a book about his experiences as a child soldier and travels the world speaking about global issues. Jal founded Gua Africa, a charity that provides educational programs for children affected by war in East Africa.

> Children represent the future of any country. Without healthy, educated children, a country's hope for the future will never be realized.

> *...the importance of education to me is what I'm willing to die for. I'm willing to die for this, because I know what it can do to my people.*
>
> EMMANUEL JAL,
> TED TALK: THE MUSIC OF A WAR CHILD, MARCH 2014

Rehabilitation

There are three key steps to help guide former child soldiers through rehabilitation and reintegration into their communities. First, whenever possible, they should be reunited with their families. If their family accepts them back, the surrounding community will likely do the same. They need to feel accepted and worthy of love.

Medical Treatment

Medical treatment must be available to treat any war-related injuries or illnesses, such as HIV/AIDS or malaria. Girls who have been subjected to sexual abuse may need special medical attention.

Psychological counseling can provide children with a safe space to discuss their trauma and rebuild their sense of self-worth and identity. They will need to learn to cope in what may continue to be a dangerous environment.

Chapter Five: Rehabilitation and Reintegration

> *Their past cannot be changed, but their future can.*
>
> "Child Soldiers," ICRC, August 2012

Education

Education is the third key step to building a better future. Children need to return to school. It can help children become motivated and confident. Education and skills training can break the cycle of poverty and violence. They can help children feel empowered to create a positive future for themselves and their families.

A young man displaced by conflict gets skilled trades training at the Kakuma refugee camp in Kenya, East Africa. Kakuma was established in 1992 by the Kenyan government and the United Nations High Commissioner for Refugees (UNHCR). Kenya has announced plans to close the camp, despite the ongoing need.

Who Is There to Help?

Organizations such as UNICEF and the International Committee of the Red Cross/Red Crescent partner with government and community groups. They try to address the reasons for child recruitment and work to prevent it. They connect families and their children—former child soldiers—to health services, schools, and skills training.

Since 1998, UNICEF has helped more than 100,000 former child soldiers reintegrate into their communities.

Chapter Five: Rehabilitation and Reintegration

Amnesty International (AI) campaigns for a world in which human rights are a fundamental right shared by everyone. It raises money a number of ways, including donations from people all over the world.

Other organizations are dedicated to eliminating the use of child soldiers through awareness campaigns and rescue and rehabilitation programs. War Child is an organization dedicated to a future in which no child's life is devastated by war. It is committed to supporting former child soldiers on their path to a better future.

AI documents violations of international law during armed conflicts. It also works to secure the release of children recruited as soldiers, as well as providing them with support once they are released.

Wrap-Up

Looking to the Future

The simplest way to protect children from being recruited as child soldiers would be to prevent conflicts from ever taking place.

If this is unlikely, then we will need more effective tools to hold governments, armed forces, and other groups accountable for their actions in recruiting child soldiers. We also need to partner with communities to address the root causes of violence against children.

With so many problems in the world, it can feel overwhelming. Often, people can only focus on one problem at a time.

> *Peace remains the best protection for children affected by armed conflict.*
>
> António Guterres, UN Secretary-General, UN News, July 2019

Better education and opportunities for a brighter future will help children and their families resist the appeal of armed groups and the promises—of food, shelter, and security—that they offer. There are many causes or motivations for conflict. Poverty and poor or unstable governments are two that threaten the lives of children and their families. These often lead to the recruitment of child soldiers. Education is one way to help lessen or end poverty. Supporting good and strong governments that have laws that aid all citizens can help prevent some conflicts.

Syrian refugee children study at a refugee camp in Turkey. Civil war has raged in Syria since 2011. It has led to massacres, mass destruction, and displaced people.

Young people gather to speak out about conflict in Afghanistan. Protesting is important, but being informed and pressing your government for action is also important.

What Can You Do?

You can help by supporting efforts to eliminate the use of child soldiers around the world. Stay informed about the issue. Talk with your friends and family to spread awareness about it. Take part in events that draw attention to issues such as war and its impact on children. Welcome newcomers in your community who may have fled conflict areas. Learn about your community's commitment to provide safe places for them.

Most people who escape war to live in refugee camps never get resettled in other countries. Growing up in a refugee camp deprives children of opportunities.

Wrap-Up: Looking to the Future

PERSPECTIVES

FEBRUARY 12

RED HAND DAY

Red Hand Day

Red Hand Day was created in 2002 and takes place every year on February 12. It is also called International Day Against the Use of Child Soldiers. Hundreds of thousands of red handprints have been collected from more than 50 countries over the years to highlight the challenges faced by children who have returned home from conflicts. The campaign asks governments to support efforts to end the practice of using children in conflicts.

A memorial at a war protest

> *Every child deserves the opportunity to play, laugh and learn; to explore and grow in a world that nurtures them.*
>
> "CHILD SOLDIER: FROM WAR TO RECOVERY," UNICEF CANADA, FEBRUARY 2019

GLOSSARY

cartel A group that works to illegally control the price of a product

commander A person who has authority or power over a group of people

deliberate Something done on purpose

desensitized Made less likely to feel shock or pain

enforcers People who impose their will on others by using violence or intimidation

indocrinate To teach people to accept beliefs uncritically or without question

infamous Well known for bad behavior or actions

manipulate To control someone or something in a skillful way

militant Using strong or extreme methods to achieve something

militia A group of soldiers who are local citizens and not part of the regular army

minority A smaller group of people, often from a different community or race who are commonly discriminated against

Nazi beliefs The beliefs of the Nazi Party, including a strong or authoritarian state and military, and the superiority of certain white, European races

paramilitary An unofficial military force of a country

political systems The kind of government a country has, such as a democracy or an authoritarian state

protocol Official rules or procedures for running something such as a country

radicalization The process of causing someone to adopt extreme views and attitudes

recruit To enlist or admit someone into the armed forces or armed groups

refugee Someone who has been forced to leave their country because of war or violence

rehabilitate To help someone return to a healthy or normal way of living

reintegrate To restore or bring something back to a larger group

stigmas Negative and often unfair beliefs about something

World War I A major war in Europe and parts of the Middle East, Asia, and Africa from 1914 to 1918

World War II A major war from 1939 to 1945 between the Allies and the Axis powers

STAY INFORMED

Child Soldiers and You

The United Nations says one in six children in the world live in areas affected by war and armed conflict. Children are never responsible for armed conflict but they are harmed by its violence. Children do not choose to be soldiers. They are forced by circumstances. What can you do to help child soldiers?

1. Read and learn more about the reasons children become soldiers.
2. Understand how conflicts and wars impact children.
3. Learn what your country and aid agencies are doing to help child soldiers.
4. Share what you have learned with other people.

Books to Read

Chikwanine, Michel, and Jessica Dee Humphreys. *Child Soldier: When Boys and Girls Are Used in War.* Kids Can Press, 2015.

Duany, Ger, and Garen Thomas. *Walk Toward the Rising Sun: From Child Soldier to Ambassador of Peace.* Make Me a World, 2020.

McKay, Sharon E., and Daniel Lafrance. *War Brothers: The Graphic Novel.* Annick Press, 2013.

Websites to Visit

https://imyourneighborbooks.org

This website encourages community conversation about immigration, welcoming, and community building through books for children and youths. Subjects include child soldiers, conflict, refugees, and immigration.

https://www.icrc.org/en/doc/assets/files/other/icrc-002-0824.pdf

This International Committee of the Red Cross brief is a publication that gives useful information about the organization's work with child soldiers.

https://www.unicef.org/child-rights-convention/convention-text-childrens-version

This website provides a child-friendly version of the United Nations Convention on the Rights of the Child.

INDEX

—A—
American Civil War 6
Amnesty International 41
Anywar, Ricky Richard 12

—B—
Beah, Ishmael 17, 31
Bensouda, Fatou 29
Boko Haram 19

—C—
cartels 7

—D—
Dallaire, Roméo 11, 33
desensitization 13, 16, 17
drug dependency 13, 16, 17, 31

—E—
education 37, 39, 43

—G—
gender-based violence 13, 38
Geneva Conventions 22–23

—H—
Hitler Youth 6, 20
Hussein, Saddam 21

—I—
indoctrination 6, 16, 20
International Criminal Court (ICC) 27, 28, 29
Iraq 21, 35
ISIS 35

—J—
Jal, Emmanuel 37

—K—
Kony, Joseph 21

—M—
militants 12, 19
militia 5, 20, 33

—N—
Nazi Party 6, 20
Nuremberg trials 22

—P—
paramilitary 21
patriotism 15, 16
post-traumatic stress disorder (PTSD) 31, 33

—R—
radicalization 11
rebels 4, 5, 11, 17–20, 28
recruitment 5, 7, 8, 10, 11, 14–21, 23–29, 34, 35, 40–43
Red Cross/Red Crescent 26, 40
Red Hand Day 45
rehabilitation and reintegration 12, 17, 32, 36–41

—S—
sexual assault 13, 38

—T—
trauma 13, 30, 31, 32, 36, 37, 38

—U—
UNICEF 40
United Nations Convention on the Rights of the Child (UNCRC) 24–25

—W—
War Child 41
war crimes 22, 27, 29, 34
warlords 21
World War I (WWI) 7, 8, 9, 15
World War II (WWII) 6, 20, 22, 23

—Y—
Yemen 5, 31, 36

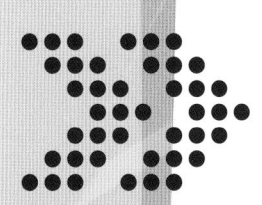

About the Author
Linda Barghoorn has traveled to more than 60 countries and shared experiences and adventures with extraordinary people. She believes that learning about people, places, and things can teach us a lot about ourselves and how we can change the world to make it a better place for all.